THE CAR-BUYING FORMULA

MADE EASY

AUTHOR: HARVEY BROWN

$$e^{i\pi} + 1 = 0$$

COPYRIGHT

$$e^{i\pi} + 1 = 0$$

BIOGRAPHY

Selling cars is my life. I've been in the car industry for 15 years now. I have been a top salesperson for as long as I can remember. My knack for sales led me to an opportunity in car sales that changed my life. It all started with my first car purchase. As I walked onto the parking lot, I was outwardly confident, but on the inside, I didn't have the slightest idea of what would become of my visit. As I exited the car, the salesperson greeted me with a smile and sold me a Ford Taurus Limited Edition. I couldn't believe it. I was so excited walking out of the showroom with my new car keys that I could hardly contain myself.

I remember asking myself where I would go and what I would do now that I had reliable transportation. I was doing well for myself, working for a huge company that has been around forever. This particular company — I won't name it — paid me very well at the time for a sales job, which I

$$e^{i\pi} + 1 = 0$$

excelled at because I'm a bit of a natural in sales. Then came the day my whole world crashed; I got laid off due to a company-wide closing. "I wasn't expecting that!" I then had to think fast. "Oh, there's a job fair coming up

soon. Maybe I'll go check it out," I thought. When I arrived, everyone was smiling and mingling while passing out resumes. I felt naked because I didn't bring my resume along, but I didn't even have one to bring.

As I was walking around and watching everyone else laughing and having fun, I ran into a familiar face. It was my car salesman. I said, "What are you doing here?" He said, "I'm representing the dealership, and I'm the manager now."

Then I said, "Get out of here - good for you, congratulations." He then proceeded to ask me why I was there, so I told him my sob story about the company closing.

After listening to me, he asked if I had sales experience. I answered, "Are you kidding me? Sales experience is like my middle name."

$$e^{i\pi} + 1 = 0$$

He laughed, gave me his business card, and told me I could start on Monday. And as they say, the rest is history. Since then, in my time selling cars, I've made the highest sales countless times in most months and been the salesman of the year at every dealership I worked at.

I have compiled a list of this book's most frequently asked questions sprinkled with <u>seasoned</u> tips from the pros. After reading this book, you will be equipped with the preparation to give you the confidence to make a sound-informed decision in buying a car.

Thank you, and I hope you enjoy it. Sincerely, Harvey SalesExperience Brown

$$e^{i\pi} + 1 = 0$$

From Imagination to Creation… Crafted with Words, Art, and Passion

Written, Designed, Promo Video Created, Narrated, and Brought to Life by Shujath Hussain

ISBN:

Edition:

$$e^{i\pi} + 1 = 0$$

PREFACE

Welcome to "The Car Buying Formula: Made Easy" – your go-to guide for mastering the art of purchasing automobiles like a pro. This book will equip you with the knowledge and strategies to confidently navigate the car buying process and secure the best deal possible.

> **Empowering Yourself with Information:**

Research is vital: Take the time to research different car models, pricing strategies, and dealership reputations to negotiate like a pro.

Know your needs: Understand what you need in a car to avoid unnecessary extras and focus on your priorities.

Understand financing: Educate yourself about financing options to secure the most favorable deal.

> **Building Your Arsenal of Leverage:**

Confidence is critical: Cultivate confidence to assert your value as a customer and negotiate effectively.

Timing matters: Identify the best times to buy based on market trends to maximize your advantage.

$$e^{i\pi} + 1 = 0$$

Research dealerships: Choose reputable dealerships that prioritize customer satisfaction.

> **Sealing the Deal:**

Schedule a test drive: Schedule a test drive in advance to assess the vehicle and negotiate from a position of strength.

Get pre-approved: Secure pre-approval for financing to demonstrate your commitment and streamline the buying process.

Negotiate effectively: Come prepared with research and clear boundaries to negotiate a win-win deal.

With these strategies, you're ready to embark on your car-buying journey with confidence and success. Let's get started!

$$e^{i\pi} + 1 = 0$$

TABLE OF CONTENTS

$$e^{i\pi} + 1 = 0$$

$$e^{i\pi} + 1 = 0$$

INTRODUCTION

Hello, car shoppers! Welcome to the realm of negotiating for automobiles. In this section, we will explore the skill of making informed choices. Uncover the strategies that will give you an unbeatable edge in dealing with dealerships. By equipping yourself with the knowledge and these resources, you can approach the showroom like a pro, ready to overcome any challenge and drive off in your dream car. Let's jump in and discover how you can become a master at leveraging your position and tapping into your brilliance when buying a car.

EMPOWERING YOURSELF WITH INFORMATION

➢ **The Power of Research**

$$e^{i\pi} + 1 = 0$$

To successfully navigate purchasing a car, you must empower yourself with this valuable tool: knowledge. Take your time to investigate every facet of your car-buying journey thoroughly. Investigate everything from car models and their unique attributes to pricing strategies and the reputations of local dealerships. By doing so, you will be equipped with the insights to negotiate like a seasoned professional.

> ### **Identifying Your Needs and Wants**

Before going to the dealership, it's essential to have a clear understanding of your needs and preferences. Are you looking for a fuel-efficient vehicle that suits your daily commute, or do you need a sturdy SUV to handle off-road adventures?

Knowing what you require will help you to stay focused and avoid being influenced by unnecessary extras.

> ### Understanding Financing Options

Understanding the importance of financing in a deal is

$$e^{i\pi} + 1 = 0$$

crucial. Find the time to educate yourself about the available options. Look into interest rates, lease terms, and alternative ways of financing. By being well-informed and prepared, you can secure the most favourable deal possible, ultimately saving yourself a significant amount of money.

BUILDING YOUR ARSENAL OF LEVERAGE

➢ Cultivating an Aura of Confidence

Having confidence is crucial when entering the arena of negotiations. It's essential to firmly believe in your value as a customer and your capacity to walk away if the deal doesn't align with your needs. By demonstrating your determination, dealerships will understand that you are serious and will be motivated to fulfil your requirements.

➢ Timing is Everything

The car buying landscape is influenced by seasons, holidays, and sales events. By identifying the best time to strike, you

$$e^{i\pi} + 1 = 0$$

can harness the power of market trends to your advantage. Be patient, be strategic, and strike when the iron is hot.

➢ Researching Local Dealership Reputations

Having the right information is crucial when it comes to choosing a dealership partner. Take the time to research their reputation, seek recommendations and discover trustworthy establishments that may be hidden gems. It's important to align yourself with a dealership that has a good reputation and is willing to go above and beyond to earn your business.

SEALING THE DEAL

➢ Timing Your Test Drive

Walk onto the dealership lot with swagger and magnify your presence by scheduling a test drive in advance. This positions you as a serious buyer worthy of the dealer's utmost attention. Use this opportunity to assess the vehicle's condition, handling, and any potential flaws that might further sway

$$e^{i\pi} + 1 = 0$$

negotiations.

➢ **Utilizing the Power of Pre-Approval**

When you head to the dealership, make sure you have a pre-approval for financing in hand. This is a great advantage as it shows the dealer that you are committed, have good credit scores and are prepared to finalize the purchase. It helps remove any doubts, speeds up the process and allows you to concentrate on finding the ideal vehicle.

➢ **Mastering the Art of Negotiation**

Negotiating is like a graceful dance and as the buyer, you have the upper hand. When you're entering a negotiation, come prepared with your research, clear boundaries and a determination to achieve your desired outcome. It's important to be assertive but maintain a friendly atmosphere, working towards a win-win situation that satisfies both parties.

Well done to all you smart car buyers out there! By becoming

$$e^{i\pi} + 1 = 0$$

skilled at making informed decisions, you've unlocked the key to success in the overwhelming world of buying cars. With knowledge in your pocket, confident negotiation skills and unwavering determination, you're now ready to step onto the dealership floor and leave as a triumphant car buying champion. Embrace the challenge ahead, remember that leverage is on your side and get ready to celebrate your well deserved victory. Prepare yourself for an amazing ride as you unleash your inner genius in buying cars and drive away in the vehicle of your dreams.

$$e^{i\pi} + 1 = 0$$

CHAPTER 1

UNDERSTANDING YOUR NEEDS AND BUDGET
THE FOUNDATION OF UNLOCKING THE KEYS TO SUCCESS

$$e^{i\pi} + 1 = 0$$

UNLEASH YOUR INNER CAR BUYING GENIUS

Greetings, fellow car enthusiasts and welcome to the beginning of your quest to become a savvy car buyer. In this first chapter, we will thoroughly explore the vital elements of comprehending your requirements and financial situation. By establishing a strong foundation, you will be equipped to make well informed choices when it comes to buying your dream car. Get ready to unleash your expertise in car purchasing as we delve into the fascinating relationship between your individual lifestyle, desires and financial means.

DEFINING YOUR LIFESTYLE

$$e^{i\pi} + 1 = 0$$

Visualize yourself embarking on a voyage. Where do you want to explore? Who will join you as your travel mate? What feelings will have a hold of you? It's necessary to recognize your way of life and wishes to get the best car for yourself. Are you a resident in the city who needs a car to weave through roads and yet stylish and fuel conservative at the same time? Or are you the one who likes thrilling escapades, needing an SUV to carry all your requirement and also a mighty drive to roam through nature? Allot some time and contemplate on your wants and lifestyle to start your voyage to the right car.

PRIORITIZING YOUR NEEDS

Must-Haves and Deal Breakers

Now that you have an understanding of your car preferences, it's crucial to determine the features and functions that you

$$e^{i\pi} + 1 = 0$$

absolutely need. Take some time to create a list of negotiable factors such as, the number of passengers you usually transport, the desired safety features, specific technological advancements you're seeking, required storage space and any specialized requirements. By identifying your priorities from the start, you can efficiently narrow down your options. Avoid being swayed by unnecessary choices, along the journey.

ASSESSING YOUR BUDGET

The Financial Roadmap

When it comes to buying a car, it's not about satisfying your desires; it also involves aligning your spending with your financial goals. Before you begin the car buying process, take a moment to assess your budget. Consider your income, expenses and long term objectives. Are you willing to stretch your budget for the car you've always dreamed of or would you prefer a more financially responsible option that allows for savings or investment opportunities? Crunch the numbers,

$$e^{i\pi} + 1 = 0$$

evaluate your commitments and establish a realistic budget that empowers you rather than restricts you.

CALCULATING YOUR AFFORDABILITY

The Power of Pre-Approval

Knowing how much you can afford goes beyond being aware of your income and expenses. It involves understanding your capacity. By going through the process of getting pre-approved for a car loan, you gain knowledge about your purchasing ability. This empowers you to make informed decisions that align with what you can afford. Take the initiative to reach out to lenders and financial institutions to secure your pre- approval, taking into account factors like interest rates, loan terms and down payment requirements.

This step by step financial guide will light the way towards achieving success in buying your car.

$$e^{i\pi} + 1 = 0$$

BEWARE THE HIDDEN COSTS

Unmasking the Truth

$$e^{i\pi} + 1 = 0$$

As you delve deeper into the process of purchasing a car, it's important to keep in mind that there may be hidden expenses lurking beneath the surface. While the price tag of the car may appear affordable, at a glance there are costs to consider such as insurance, fuel, maintenance and potential repairs. These expenses can quickly put a strain on your stability. It's crucial to research and understand the cost of owning your desired vehicle, taking into account factors like fuel efficiency, insurance rates and average maintenance expenditures. By uncovering the truth about these hidden costs, you'll be able to make decisions that protect your budget from financial burdens in the future.

HARNESS THE POWER OF NEGOTIATION

Becoming a Shrewd Master

$$e^{i\pi} + 1 = 0$$

Now that you have an understanding of your needs and budget, it's time to dive into the art of negotiation. Negotiation is not just for a few people; it's a skill that every person looking to buy a car can and should develop. Take the initiative to visit dealerships, compare prices and use your research as leverage to get the best possible deal. By negotiating the price, interest rates and additional perks, it can significantly impact how affordable your dream car becomes. Mastering this skill will not save you money but also give you an advantage in the car buying process.

Your Journey Begins Now.

Well done fellow car buyers! You're well on your way to becoming a car shopper. By understanding your needs and budget, you have laid a foundation that will guide you through the complex world of car buying. You now have an idea of what your lifestyle demands entail, have prioritized your requirements accurately, assessed your budget and

$$e^{i\pi} + 1 = 0$$

uncovered any costs.

With the power of negotiation at your fingertips, you are fully prepared to embark on your journey to purchase a carwith confidence and authority.

Remember that knowledge is key. You possess the tools to unlock the secrets of successful car buying. Get ready to masterthe game, secure the car you've been dreaming of and hit the road with a sense of accomplishment and satisfaction.

Stay tuned for our installment where we'll delve into in depth research and preparation to ensure your car buying experienceis fulfilling.

So fasten your seatbelts, my friends—a thrilling and rewardingadventure awaits!

$$e^{i\pi} + 1 = 0$$

CHAPTER 2

EMPOWER YOURSELF WITHONLINE TOOLSINFORMATION
THAT WILL TAKE YOU FAR

$$e^{i\pi} + 1 = 0$$

$$e^{i\pi} + 1 = 0$$

Welcome to Chapter 2 of *"The Car Buying Formula: Made Easy."* In this captivating chapter, we will explore the realm of resources and websites that can assist you in becoming a car buying expert. Similar to a driver on a race track, these priceless tools will equip you with the knowledge needed to make informed decisions and accelerate your journey towards your triumph in buying a car . So prepare yourself for an adventure, car buyers, as we tap into our innate expertise inthe world of purchasing automobiles.

Are you prepared to fully leverage the internet's potential and take your car buying adventure to new heights? Similar to how expert drivers rely on their team for crucial information and support, these online tools and websites can provide you with the knowledge and confidence necessary to navigate through the car buying process successfully. Fasten your seat belts as we explore the top essential websites and

$$e^{i\pi} + 1 = 0$$

online resources that will transform you into a savvy car buyer.

NEVER OVER PAY FOR A NEW CAR

The Great Equalizer

With *TRUEcar*, you can gain access to a revolutionary tool that enables you to shop **WHOLESALE** prices with different dealerships for new cars. By comparing prices from multiple dealers, you can ensure that you're getting the best possible deal for your dream car. With *TRUEcar*, you have the power to negotiate with confidence, armed with the knowledge of the average price paid by other buyers in your area. Say goodbye to uncertainty and hello to your successful and calculated car buying journey!

https://www.truecar.com

$$e^{i\pi} + 1 = 0$$

VALIDATE PUBLIC DATA

When You Know, You Know

Next up, we have *true people* search, a tool that helps complete the personal information needed to complete references for the lender. One of the crucial components of the car buying process is securing financing. To get the best rates and terms, lenders often require references to verify your identity, address, and other personal information. *True people* search **enables you** to quickly and easily find and verify this information, ensuring a smooth financing process. With *true people* search, you can provide the lender with the necessary references, thus **building trust and credibility** in your loan application.

https://www.truepeoplesearch.com/ Consumer Reviews

$$e^{i\pi} + 1 = 0$$

THE TURBOCHARGER OF KNOWLEDGE

$$e^{i\pi} + 1 = 0$$

Consumer reviews are incredibly valuable when it comes to making decisions about vehicles. Websites such as *Consumer Reports* and *Edmunds,* provide in depth reviews from car owners giving insights into reliability, performance and overall satisfaction. These reviews offer a perspective on the ownership experience. They can help you avoid any potential issues. Think of them as a turbocharger for your knowledge, thus boosting your confidence as you move forward in your car buying journey.

https://www.consumerreports.org

https://www.edmunds.com/car-reviews

LATEST BANK RATES

Shift into the Financing Gear

When it comes to buying a car, it's important to stay informed about the interest rates offered by banks. Websites such as *Bankrate* and *LendingTree* give you access to up to date rates from lenders. By comparing these rates and terms, you can find the best financing options available. Remember, getting the financing is a crucial step in your car purchase journey and by focusing on securing favorable terms, you are taking charge of your financial success.

https://www.bankrate.com/search/

CAR PAYMENT CALCULATOR

Calculate Your Way into Chasing Dreams

To make sure that the car you plan to buy is affordable for you, it's essential to use a car payment calculator. Websites such as *Bankrate* and *Edmunds* provide calculators that help you estimate your monthly payments based on factors like the duration of the loan down payment, interest rate and trade value. By using this tool, you can find the balance that

$$e^{i\pi} + 1 = 0$$

matches your financial objectives and dreams.

https://www.edmunds.com/car-reviews

https://www.bankrate.com

BOOK VALUE

Fuel Your Negotiation Power

Negotiating the price of a car can be an intense battle, but armed with the knowledge of the book value, you become an informed warrior. Websites like *Kelley Blue Book* and *NADA Guides,* provide comprehensive vehicle pricing information, including the trade-in value, private party value, and retail value. By knowing the book value of the car you're interested in, **you gain an advantage** during negotiations, thus ensuring you get a fair deal.

https://www.kbb.com/

https://www.nada.org/

$e^{i\pi} + 1 = 0$

TOWING GUIDE CAPACITY

Tow Your Way to Adventure

For those seeking adventure or needing towing capabilities, **knowing** the towing guide capacity of various vehicles is vital. Websites like *Camping World Towing Guide* offer comprehensive guides that provide towing capacities, including weight limits and other additional equipment necessary for towing. By understanding the towing capabilities of different vehicles, you can choose the one that suits your needs and venture into new horizons with confidence.

https://rv.campingworld.com/towguide

$$e^{i\pi} + 1 = 0$$

MILES PER GALLON (MPG)

Efficiency is Fuel for Your Wallet

Saving money on fuel expenses is always a smart move. Websites like *FuelEconomy.gov* provide reliable information on the miles per gallon (MPG) for various vehicle models. By considering the MPG of prospective cars, you can estimate your fuel costs and make a financially wise decision. *Remember, efficiency is the fuel for your wallet.*

TRIM LEVEL PACKAGE DESCRIPTION

Customize Your Victory Lap

When you're looking at a car model, it's important to have an understanding of the various trim levels and package options. Websites such as the manufacturers site or *Edmunds,* offer explanations of these trim levels, including the features, specifications and choices available. By personalizing your victory lap with the trim level and package you can ensure that

$$e^{i\pi} + 1 = 0$$

your car perfectly aligns with your desires and requirements.

https://www.edmunds.com

FUTURE VALUE ESTIMATOR

Calculate Your Long-Term Success

Thinking about the **long-term value** of your purchase is a keyaspect of buying a car. Websites

likethe *undeniable powerhouse of car buying tools* and *Kelley Blue Book,* offer future value estimators which allow you to estimate the potential depreciation of your chosen vehicle over time. Bycalculating your long-term success, you can make a more informed decision about the car's potential value in the future. https://www.kbb.com

$$e^{i\pi} + 1 = 0$$

VEHICLE IDENTIFICATION NUMBER (VIN) DECODER

Unlock the Mystery

Understanding the details contained in the Vehicle Identification Number (VIN) can be a valuable resource. Popular websites like *Carfax* and *AutoCheck,* provide tools to VINs, giving you access to comprehensive vehicle history reports. Through VIN decoding, you can discover information such as past accidents, ownership records and service history.Equipped with this knowledge, you'll be able to make an confident choice regarding the condition of the vehicle. https://www.carfax.com

https://www.autocheck.com

WINDOW STICKER LOOK UP

Uncover the Car's Secrets

Ever wanted to know the **exact specifications** and **features** of a vehicle based on its VIN? Websites like *Window*

$$e^{i\pi} + 1 = 0$$

Sticker Look Up allow you to search for a car's **original window sticker** by entering its VIN. This reveals the car's original specifications, including the manufacturer's suggested retail price (MSRP). By uncovering the car's **secrets**, you can verify its authenticity and compare it with the seller's claims.

https://windowstickerlookup.com

CARFAX

The Comprehensive Background Check

Performing a comprehensive background check on a used car is crucial to **avoid potential risks**. *Carfax* is a **trusted** website that provides detailed vehicle history reports based on the car's VIN. These reports include valuable information such as reported accidents, odometer readings, title information, and more. By utilizing *Carfax*, you can have your peace of mind knowing that you have a complete

$$e^{i\pi} + 1 = 0$$

picture of the car's history.

https://www.carfax.com

MANHEIM VALUE

Set Your Buying Strategy

If you're looking to take part in auctions or want to get an idea of the worth of a car, platforms such as *Manheim Value* provide tools for pricing and valuation. With *Manheim Value,* you can estimate the market value of a vehicle by considering its condition, mileage and other relevant factors. By utilizing the insights from *Manheim Value* to shape your purchasing strategy, you can confidently decide on the price you're comfortable paying.

https://site.manheim.com

ORIGINAL MSRP

Know the Manufacturer's Intent

$$e^{i\pi} + 1 = 0$$

Understanding the original manufacturer's suggested retail price (MSRP) empowers you during car negotiations. Websites like *Edmunds* and *TrueCar* provide access to historical MSRP data for both new and used vehicles. By highlighting the original price set by the manufacturer, you gain valuable insight into the vehicle's value and can **negotiate effectively**. *https://www.truecar.com*

https://www.edmunds.com

COMPLIMENTARY RELATED WEBSITES

Beyond the Finish Line

In addition to the essential websites mentioned above, there are numerous complimentary websites that can enhance your car buying experience. Websites like *AutoTrader, Cars.com,* and *CarGurus,* offer comprehensive vehicle listings with advanced search filters. These websites allow you to find the perfect car based on your desired make, model, year, price,

$$e^{i\pi} + 1 = 0$$

and location. Additionally, websites like *Jalopnik* and *MotorTrend* provide both engaging and informative content that can further fuel your passion for cars.

https://www.cars.com

https://www.cargurus.com

https://jalopnik.com

https://www.motortrend.com

Congratulations! You have now been equipped with the best essential websites and online tools to excel in your car buying journey. By utilizing these tools, you unleash your inner car buying genius, thus gaining the knowledge and confidence needed to make informed decisions. Consumer reviews turbocharge your knowledge, while latest bank rates, shift you into the financing gear. The car payment calculator helps you calculate your way to chasing dreams, and the book value fuels your negotiation power. Towing guide capacity empowers you to tow your way to adventure, while

$$e^{i\pi} + 1 = 0$$

MPG serves as the efficiency fuel for your wallet. You can customize your victory lap with trim level package descriptions and calculate your long-term success with future value estimators.

The VIN decoder unlocks the mystery, driver's license checks ensure that you drive with confidence, and window sticker look-up uncovers the car's secrets. *Carfax* provides a comprehensive background check, *Manheim Value* sets your buying strategy, and original MSRP sheds light on the manufacturer's intent. Along the way, numerous complimentary websites broaden your car buying horizons, thus ensuring a fulfilling and successful journey.

So rev up your engines, my fellow car buyers, and utilize these online tools and websites to unleash your inner car buying genius. Remember, you have the power to conquer the car buying track with knowledge, confidence, and a thirst for adventure.

$$e^{i\pi} + 1 = 0$$

CHAPTER 3

RESEARCHING THE DEALERSHIPS UNLEASHING YOUR INNER CAR BUYING GENIUS

$$e^{i\pi} + 1 = 0$$

$$e^{i\pi} + 1 = 0$$

Welcome car buyers, to the exciting and pivotal second chapter of your journey to mastering the car buying formula. In this installment, we will navigate through the treacherous terrain of dealership selection, thus transforming you into a savvy car buyer armed with the knowledge needed to make the best possible decision. Prepare to dive deep into the world of research and come out on top, ready to unleash your inner car buying genius.

KNOW WHAT YOU WANT

Defining Your Buying Criteria

Before you begin your search for the dealership, pause for a moment to establish your purchasing standards. What aspects are most important to you? Is it transparency, outstanding

$$e^{i\pi} + 1 = 0$$

customer service or a diverse array of vehicles? Remember to take your preferences into account and compile a list of non negotiable factors. By being aware of your desires, you can concentrate on your investigations and reach an educated judgement that aligns with your purchasing criteria.

HARNESS THE POWER OF THE INTERNET

Seek and You Shall Find

The internet becomes your greatest ally when searching for the ideal car dealership. With just a few clicks, an abundance of information becomes readily available to you. Utilize search engines to locate dealerships near your location and browse through their websites. Seek out dealerships that are open about their pricing, boast positive customer reviews and present a diverse range of vehicles that align with your requirements. Make note of any accolades or awards they have earned, as it signifies their excellence in the industry.

$$e^{i\pi} + 1 = 0$$

TAP INTO WORD-OF-MOUTH

The Power of Recommendations

Don't underestimate the power of recommendations—tap into the network of car buyers you trust. Ask friends, family members, and co-workers about their experiences with various dealerships. Learn from their triumphs and mishaps, gaining valuable insights to avoid potential pitfalls. Take note of any recurring recommendations—those dealerships that consistently receive positive feedback are likely worth considering.

VISIT DEALERSHIPS IN PERSON

Assessing the Experience

No car purchasing journey is really complete without taking a test drive. It's an opportunity to evaluate both the vehicle itself and the dealerships dedication to your satisfaction.

$$e^{i\pi} + 1 = 0$$

Once you've narrowed down your choices, it's crucial to visit thedealerships in person. Take note of things when assessing yourexperience and ensure that you remain in control of your car buying instincts. Pay attention to the appearance of the dealership—is it clean and well maintained? Also observe how the staff is dressed and their professionalism. Engage with the sales team by asking them questions about pricing, financing options and any incentives that may be available. Watch closelyfor their responses—are they open and transparent. Do they seem evasive

THE TEST DRIVE

The Ultimate Assessment

No car buying experience is truly complete, without taking a test drive. It's an opportunity to evaluate both the vehicle itself and the dealerships dedication to ensuring your satisfaction[EQ2] .

$$e^{i\pi} + 1 = 0$$

Make sure to schedule test drives at your preferred dealerships and pay attention to how knowledgeable and enthusiastic the salesperson is when explaining the features and advantages of the vehicle. Take note not only of the vehicle but also how accommodating the dealership is in meeting your needs and providing a memorable experience.

Don't forget to inquire about their service department by asking questions about maintenance and post purchase support. A dealership that goes above and beyond in prioritizing your satisfaction even after the sale, is definitely worth considering – like finding a gem!

BE CONFIDENT IN YOUR CHOICE

Trust Your Inner Car Buying Genius

Equipped with knowledge, expertise and your innate car buying savvy, you are now prepared to make an informed choice. Rely on your intuition. Select a dealership that matches your purchasing criteria and offers an outstanding

$$e^{i\pi} + 1 = 0$$

buying experience. Keep in mind that you have the ability to shape your car buying adventure and with the support of the dealership, you're on track for a successful car purchase journey.

Congratulations car buyers, on mastering the art of researching dealerships! By utilizing the power of the internet, seeking recommendations from others, exploring reviews, physically visiting dealerships and conducting thorough test drives, you have paved the way for a successful car buying journey. As a car buyer, you possess the knowledge and insights necessary to make a wise decision that fulfills your requirements and surpasses your expectations.

Have faith in your instincts as a car buyer and select a dealership that aligns with your values, delivers exceptional customer service and offers vehicles that ignite your enthusiasm. Remember that the dealership you choose is not merely a place for a transaction – it serves as an entrance to a

$$e^{i\pi} + 1 = 0$$

car buying experience. Embrace the adventure, let your car buying expertise come to life and drive away with assurance knowing that you have made the decision when selecting a dealership.

Keep an eye out for the upcoming chapter, where we will delve deeper into the art of asking questions thus equipping you with the information required to secure an excellent deal. Your triumph in purchasing a car is around the corner—let your innate talent for buying a car shine brightly!

$$e^{i\pi} + 1 = 0$$

CHAPTER 4

PREPARING QUESTIONS TO ASK THE SALESPERSON:
EQUIPPING YOURSELF FOR A SUCCESSFUL CAR BUYING
JOURNEY

$$e^{i\pi} + 1 = 0$$

$$e^{i\pi} + 1 = 0$$

PREPARING QUESTIONS TO ASK THE SALESPERSON

Get ready to supercharge your expertise in buying cars and

tap into your car buying genius with, *"The Car Buying*

$$e^{i\pi} + 1 = 0$$

Formula: Made Easy." Being well prepared with a set of inquiries to ask the salesperson will assist you in gathering details and making choices. As you dive into this thrilling journey, you'll acquire the knowledge and confidence needed to navigate through the car buying process like a pro. Now is the perfect moment to take action and unlock the strategies for a car purchasing experience. Strap yourself in and prepare to accelerate towards becoming a master at buying cars!

CONSIDER THE FOLLOWING QUESTIONS TO PREPARE IN ADVANCE:

1. Can you give me an overview of the vehicles condition? I'm interested in learning about its history, including any accidents or major repairs it has undergone. This information will help me identify any issues.

2. Are there any warranties or guarantees included with the

$$e^{i\pi} + 1 = 0$$

car? I'm interested in learning about the available warranty options, what they specifically include and how long they would remain valid. Knowing the terms of the warranty will provide me with reassurance and ensure that my investment is protected.

3. Are there any fees or charges associated with the car? I want to make sure there are no costs that aren't included in the sticker price such as documentation fees, dealership fees or optional add-ons. It's important for me to have an understanding of the cost, including any additional items or charges.

CONSIDERING A TEST DRIVE AND INSPECTION OPTIONS

When it comes to assessing a vehicle's performance, comfort, condition test driving and inspecting the car are some steps to take. Here are some suggestions to keep in mind when

$$e^{i\pi} + 1 = 0$$

planning your visit to the dealership:

1. **Schedule a test drive:** It's a good idea to contact the dealership and arrange a test drive for the specific vehicles you're interested in. This way, you can evaluate how the car handles, accelerates, brakes and its overall comfort.

2. **Thoroughly inspect the vehicle:** Take your time in examining both the interior and exterior of the car for any signs of damage wear and tear or potential mechanical issues. Pay attention to whether there are any inconsistencies between what was advertised about the car's features and its actual condition.

3. **Ask for vehicle history reports:** Don't forget to request vehicle history reports like *CARFAX* or *Auto Check* from the dealership. These reports provide information about a car's past including its accident history, ownership records and service records.

By gathering all the required documents and paperwork,

$$e^{i\pi} + 1 = 0$$

setting a realistic price range for yourself, preparing some questions for the salesperson at the dealership, as well as considering your options for test driving and inspection procedures, you'll be well prepared for your visit. This level of preparation will ensure that you have an successful experience when buying a car.

$$e^{i\pi} + 1 = 0$$

CHAPTER 5

FISH OUT DEFICIENCIES ON A TEST DRIVE - BECOMING A MASTER CAR INSPECTOR

$$e^{i\pi} + 1 = 0$$

$$e^{i\pi} + 1 = 0$$

In this chapter, we will discuss how you can effectively identify any deficiencies or issues with a car while taking it for a test drive. By taking this approach, you'll have the ability to make informed choices and avoid any

$$e^{i\pi} + 1 = 0$$

complications. By becoming proficient in assessing cars, you can discover any concealed problems and increase your likelihood of finding the vehicle.

Let's delve into the realm of car inspection and unlock your inner expertise in purchasing automobiles.

PREPARATION IS KEY

Knowledge is Your Best Weapon

Prior to embarking on your test drive, it's paramount that you first complete some research. Allocate some time to compile data related specifically to the brand and model of the car which has kindled your curiosity. Stay vigilant for any potential issues or trustworthiness complexities linked with this particular vehicle. Moreover, understanding the particulars about various car elements like its engine operation, transmission functionality, suspension system and electrical integration is beneficial too. Possessing such insights could prove to be useful during the actual test driving

$$e^{i\pi} + 1 = 0$$

session as they may help in recognizing possible problems while facilitating dialogue.

VISUAL INSPECTION

The Eyes Never Lie

As you approach the vehicle, ensure to give it a comprehensive visual check. Watch out for signs of dents, scuffs or corrosion that might indicate previous collisions or neglectful upkeep. Examine closely the paint's quality, gaps in panelling and its broad external state. Review the tires for any evidence of weariness and abnormalities. Glance under the car to detect potential leaks, harm or corrosion signals. Trust your instincts as they seldom mislead you when you're observing closely. It is worthwhile in understanding its past life cycle and current status.

ROAD TEST

Feeling the Pulse of the Car

$$e^{i\pi} + 1 = 0$$

Once you're in control of the car, it's time to test its performance. It's a green signal to assess its functionality. Be aware of any out-of-the-ordinary sounds, tremors or smells that catch your attention. Notice how smoothly the car speed up, apply brakes and maneuver around corners. Does it stutter or jolt while picking up pace? Do the braking mechanics function efficiently with consistent strength throughout the drive? While driving in a straight line, does it bend towards either direction subtly but surely? Listen closely for any unnatural noise from the engine and be alert if you feel any unusual vibrations when you're running hands along the surfaces inside the cabin. These observations could prove vital in spotting potential troubles within mechanics which may not always surface right away.

COMPREHENSIVENESS IS KEY

Cover All Bases

It's vital to conduct a comprehensive review of the car

$$e^{i\pi} + 1 = 0$$

covering every aspect, in order to spot any lurking problems. All lights — headlights, brake lights and indicators — need stringent testing for optimal operation. Don't overlook trying out comfort features such as the windshield wipers or the climate control system either. It is equally important not to ignore the state of your infotainment system; audit its sound quality, navigation function and compatibility options thoroughly. Lastly but significantly, scrutinize its interior details—an existence of tears, stains or wear signs shouldn't go unnoticed. A detailed inspection routine conducted efficiently will curtail missing potential issues.

GET TECHNICAL

Scanning for Hidden Issues

While your personal insights prove to be meaningful, capitalize on contemporary tech to probe for possibly unobserved complications. Ponder employing an OBD-II scanner to assess the auto's diagnostic codes. This gadget can

$$e^{i\pi} + 1 = 0$$

expose any hidden mechanical or electrical challenges that might not be apparent at a first glance. It is indeed a resource that every proficient vehicle examiner ought to possess.

PROFESSIONAL INSPECTION

Seeking Expert Advice

Should you continue to harbor doubts about the car's state, contemplating expert intervention may be wise. A scheduled pre-purchase examination at a trusted auto shop can provide an in-depth evaluation of your prospective purchase. The comprehensive scrutiny includes test driving, meticulous inspection and requisite diagnostic tests carried out by adep mechanics. This impartial advice gifts you with assurance while saving you from the potential hefty future repair costs —truly a nominal investment worth making.

TRUST YOUR GUT

Honoring Your Intuition

$$e^{i\pi} + 1 = 0$$

In the process of buying a car, factual data and objective evaluations are indeed significant. However, do not discount your gut instincts' potential power. As you test drive the automobile and scrutinize its parts, be mindful of what your intuition tells you. Does an aura of certainty and calm envelope you? Does anything spark worries within you? In such journeys involving car purchases where specialized inspections may overlook some faults, following that instinctive hunch becomespertinent.

Congratulations! By mastering the art of identifying flaws during a test drive, you're well on your way to becoming a car inspector. Equip yourself with knowledge, conducting inspections, assessing the car's performance during the road test, utilizing technology, seeking advice if necessary and relying on your instincts. Following these strategies will provide you with the tools to spot flaws and make an informed decision.

$$e^{i\pi} + 1 = 0$$

Remember that becoming a car inspector requires practice and experience. Don't get discouraged if you initially overlook some flaws. The key is to expand your knowledge and refine your observational skills. With each test drive, you'll confidence and become better at spotting flaws. Go ahead and tap into your car buying expertise. May each test drive bring you closer to discovering the ideal car for you without any unexpected surprises along the way?

Becoming a qualified vehicle inspector demands patience, practice and experience. It's okay if you initially miss out on seeing certain defects as it is all part of the journey. The focus should be on amplifying your understanding about cars, while honing your observational skills. Each test drive will bring with it boosted confidence levels in identifying imperfections effectively—keep moving forward!

Continue to harness your knack for car assessment

$$e^{i\pi} + 1 = 0$$

during each inspection ride.When every drive is aimed at spotting potential issues, rest assured that finding an automobile perfectly suited to meet all your needs without bringing any surprise troubles along the way, becomes far more easier than every time before.

$$e^{i\pi} + 1 = 0$$

CHAPTER 6

CONQUERING THE DEALERSHIP EXPERIENCE
NAVIGATING WITH CONFIDENCE AND SAVVY

$$e^{i\pi} + 1 = 0$$

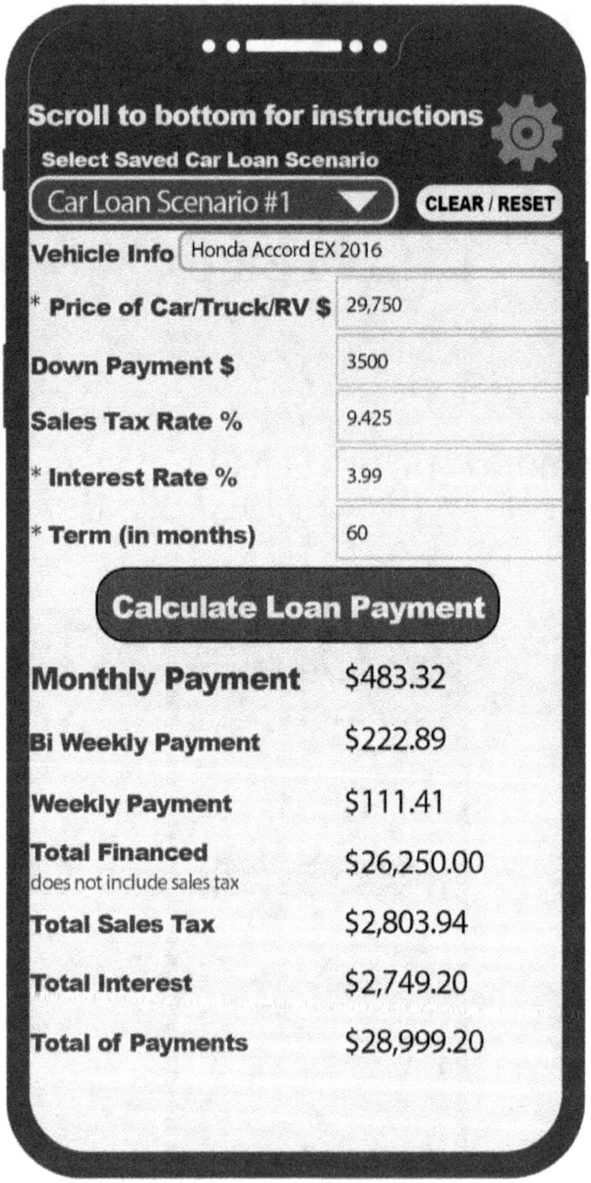

Scroll to bottom for instructions

Select Saved Car Loan Scenario

Car Loan Scenario #1   ▼   **CLEAR / RESET**

Vehicle Info Honda Accord EX 2016

*** Price of Car/Truck/RV $** 29,750

Down Payment $ 3500

Sales Tax Rate % 9.425

*** Interest Rate %** 3.99

*** Term (in months)** 60

Calculate Loan Payment

Monthly Payment $483.32

Bi Weekly Payment $222.89

Weekly Payment $111.41

Total Financed
does not include sales tax $26,250.00

Total Sales Tax $2,803.94

Total Interest $2,749.20

Total of Payments $28,999.20

$$e^{i\pi} + 1 = 0$$

WELCOME TO THE WORLD OF DEALERSHIPS

Welcome fellow car buyers, to the intriguing world of dealerships—a place where deals are made, power dynamics are at play, and your inner car buying genius will shine brightest. In this compelling chapter, we will delve into the art

$$e^{i\pi} + 1 = 0$$

of navigating the dealership experience with confidence and savvy. Get ready to conquer this unfamiliar terrain and emerge triumphantly with the best possible deal in hand.

PREPARE FOR THE SHOWDOWN

Be Armed with Knowledge

Preparing for a dealership visit is like preparing for battle—information is your most powerful weapon. Arm yourself with knowledge about the make and model of the car you desire, its market value, and any available incentives or promotions. Research the dealership's reputation, pricing strategies, and customer reviews. By being well-prepared, you will approach the dealership experience with confidence, ready to navigate through the twists and turns.

TAKE CONTROL OF THE CONVERSATION

Establish Your Dominance

$$e^{i\pi} + 1 = 0$$

As you step into the dealership, unleash your inner car buying genius and take control of the conversation. Be assertive, maintain a strong body language, and set the tone for the interaction. Remember, you are not just a customer but a car buying genius on a mission. Establish your dominance by clearly communicating your wants and needs, and don't be swayed by sales tactics. The power lies in your hands—embrace it fully.

MIND GAMES

Maintain Your Focus

Dealerships can be a labyrinth of distractions and mind games, but as a car buying genius, you possess the mental fortitude to stay focused. Beware of persuasive tactics designed to divert your attention from your objectives. Stay on track, regularly reminding yourself of your budget, must-haves, and deal breakers. Your clarity of purpose will shield you from unnecessary temptations and ensure that you

$$e^{i\pi} + 1 = 0$$

negotiate from a position of strength.

THE DANCE OF NEGOTIATION

Mastering the Back-and-Forth

Negotiation is like an intricate dance, and as a car buying genius, you must master every step. Be prepared for the back-and-forth of offer and counteroffer, maintaining your composure and displaying unwavering confidence. Use your research to challenge any inflated prices or add-on fees. Remember, negotiation is not a sign of hostility, but a necessary process to obtain the best possible deal. Embrace the dance and let your car buying genius lead the way.

TEST DRIVE WITH INTENTIONALITY

Uncover the True Potential

Taking a test drive isn't about enjoying the ride – it's a chance

$$e^{i\pi} + 1 = 0$$

to evaluate if the vehicle meets your needs. Approach the test drive with a purpose, paying attention to factors like comfort, handling and features. Feel free to ask questions and request time behind the wheel. Your aim is to discover the capabilities of the vehicle and make sure that it matches your car buying expertise. Trust your instincts and let them guide your decisionmaking process.

ENGAGE WITH MULTIPLE DEALERSHIPS

Expand Your Options

To truly master the art of buying a car, it's important not to restrict yourself to one dealership. Connect with other dealerships to broaden your options and increase your bargaining power. By exploring avenues, you'll unlock opportunities for a range of offers, incentives and alternatives. Keep in mind that the objective is not solely to secure the deal at a dealership but rather to explore all possibilities and discover the ideal match for your car buying expertise.

$$e^{i\pi} + 1 = 0$$

CHOOSE YOUR BATTLEFIELD

Online or In-person?

In this era, purchasing a car presents two options: buying online or in-person. Take some time to evaluate which approach aligns better with your preferences and current circumstances. Opting for purchases offers convenience, thus allowing you to compare prices and explore options without feeling the pressure of negotiating face-to-face. On the other hand, choosing to buy in-person offers a chance for interaction, test drives and a physical connection with the vehicle. Make your decision thoughtfully as it will shape the path for your car buying journey to thrive.

Unleash Your Inner Car Buying Genius

Congratulations fellow car buyers! You've conquered the dealership experience with confidence and savvy, unleashing

$$e^{i\pi} + 1 = 0$$

your inner car buying genius like never before. By preparing for the showdown, taking control of the conversation, maintaining focus amidst mind games, mastering the dance of negotiation, test driving with intentionality, engaging with multiple dealerships, and choosing your battlefield wisely, you have navigated through this unfamiliar terrain with grace and precision.

The dealership experience will no longer intimidate you. Armed with knowledge and unwavering confidence, you can face any dealership with the certainty that you hold the power. Embrace your inner car buying genius, and let it guide you towards the best possible deal and a satisfying car buying experience.

$$e^{i\pi} + 1 = 0$$

CHAPTER 7

THE ART OF NEGOTIATION IGNITING YOUR INNER CAR BUYING GENIUS

$$e^{i\pi} + 1 = 0$$

$$e^{i\pi} + 1 = 0$$

WELCOME TO THE THRILLING WORLD OF NEGOTIATION

Welcome fellow car buyers, to the exhilarating realm of negotiation—the key to unlocking unbeatable deals and maximizing your success in buying a car . In this electrifying

$$e^{i\pi} + 1 = 0$$

chapter, we will delve deep into the art of negotiation, equipping you with the strategies and mindset needed to unleash your inner car buying genius. Prepare to revolutionize your approach and emerge triumphant in the battle for the best possible deal.

PREPARE FOR BATTLE

Research, Research, Research

To enter the negotiation battlefield, you must arm yourself with knowledge and understanding. Begin by conducting a thorough research on the vehicle you want to purchase, its market value, and any incentives or promotions currently available. Familiarize yourself with the dealership's pricing strategies and be ready to challenge them. By being well-prepared, you will instill confidence and gain the upper hand in the negotiation process.

MASTER THE MINDSET

$$e^{i\pi} + 1 = 0$$

Confidence is Key

In the art of negotiation, mindset is everything. Embrace the mindset of a master negotiator—confident, assertive, and unyielding. Believe in the value you bring as a buyer and approach the negotiation table knowing that you deserve the best possible deal. Remember, you are not just a customer, but a skilled negotiator who refuses to settle for less than what you deserve. Let your inner car buying genius guide you towards victory.

SET YOUR IDEAL PRICE

Know Your Limits

Before you start negotiating, determine the price that you consider ideal — the amount you're willing to spend on the car you want. This price should be based on your research and what fits into your budget. Make sure you have an understanding of your limitations and don't let yourself be influenced by tactics or emotional manipulation. Stay firm in

$$e^{i\pi} + 1 = 0$$

your decision, knowing that your ideal price is both fair and reasonable. Your confidence in sticking to your budget will shape how the negotiation unfolds.

$$e^{i\pi} + 1 = 0$$

CREATE A WIN-WIN SCENARIO

Build Rapport with the Salesperson

Negotiation does not have to be a confrontational battle—instead, aim for a win-win scenario. Build rapport with the salesperson, establish a positive connection, and express your genuine interest in making a mutually beneficial deal. Show respect and understanding, and foster an atmosphere of collaboration. Remember, both parties have goals to achieve, and by working together, you can both emerge as winners.

USE THE POWER OF SILENCE

Mastering the Art of Timing

$$e^{i\pi} + 1 = 0$$

Silence is a weapon in negotiation—a powerful tool for gaining the upper hand. Learn to embrace the uncomfortable silence after making your initial offer. Do not be tempted to fill the void with unnecessary words or concessions. Let the silence work in your favor, as it often compels the other party to break and offer a counter proposal. Remember, in negotiation,patience and timing are key.

NEGOTIATE BEYOND THE PRICE

Adding Value to the Deal

Negotiating the price is one part of the equation; it's important to consider ways to enhance the deal. Take a look at opportunities to include additional value, like extended warranties, maintenance packages or extra features. Utilize your expertise and position to negotiate these added benefits thereby increasing the worth of the deal. Keep in mind that negotiations extend beyond pricing; they involve crafting a well rounded package that fulfills all of your requirements.

$$e^{i\pi} + 1 = 0$$

BE WILLING TO WALK AWAY

True Negotiating Power

One of the most potent weapons in negotiation is your willingness to walk away. Be prepared to exercise this power if the terms do not align with your expectations or goals. Show the salesperson that you have alternatives and are not desperate for their offer. This demonstration of strength can often lead to a more favorable deal as the realization of losing a customer sinks in. Remember, walking away is not a failure but a strategic move towards securing the best deal.

Unleash Your Inner Car Buying Genius

Congratulations car buyers, on mastering the art of negotiation! You have truly become a genius in the world of car buying by preparing yourself for the battle, adopting the mindset, setting your price, creating win-win situations,

$$e^{i\pi} + 1 = 0$$

understanding the power of silence, negotiating beyond just price and being willing to walk away when necessary.

As a negotiator, you have the ability to shape your car buying experience and secure the best deal possible. Trust in your research and believe in your value as you let your inner genius guide you towards victory. Remember that negotiation is not about getting the price; it's also about establishing a good relationship and adding value to both sides involved.

Stay tuned for chapter 8 where we will delve into navigating vehicle trade-ins and down payments to provide you with the skills to navigate through the final stages of your car buying journey. Your success is within reach – unleash your genius. Conquer this negotiation battlefield!

$$e^{i\pi} + 1 = 0$$

CHAPTER 8
NAVIGATING VEHICLE TRADE-INS AND DOWN PAYMENTS

$$e^{i\pi} + 1 = 0$$

ACCELERATING YOUR CAR BUYING SUCCESS

This chapter will focus on diving into the world of trade-insand down payments, revealing how you can make the most

$$e^{i\pi} + 1 = 0$$

of these strategies to enhance your car buying experience. By mastering these techniques, you'll be on the track to achieving success in buying your car. So get ready for an exhilarating rideas we unlock your car buying genius!

UNLEASHING THE POWER OF TRADE-INS

Maximizing the Value of Your Current Vehicle

If you already own a car, let's discuss the benefits of trade-ins. Trade-ins act like turbo boosters that can give you the power needed to turn your dream car into a reality. You have the ability to use the value of your vehicle towards purchasing one. However, to make the most of this opportunity, it's important to be aware of your car's market value. Don't worry because you won't need a team for this task. Websites and online resources can provide estimates based on factors such as the make, model, mileage and overall condition of your car. Equipped with this information, you'll be in control during negotiations as well as be able to figure trade-in values

$$e^{i\pi} + 1 = 0$$

foryourself.

PREPARING YOUR TRADE-IN

Showcasing Its Worth

By recognizing the worth of your vehicle, you're now prepared to put in some elbow grease and make it gleam. Bear in mind that first impressions count a lot—even when dealing with car trades. Start off by cleaning every nook and cranny of your trade-in, both inside and out. Let everyone witness how your automobile shows its sophistication and elegance. Attend to every minor imperfection such as any dents or dings that can readily be fixed or touched up neatly. Maintain routine check- ups so the quality of performance never fades over time. In doing this while showcasing your trade-in's obvious value, reinforces your leverage to negotiate a better position that will keep more dollars in the palms your hand instead of handing over all the profit to dealership.

$$e^{i\pi} + 1 = 0$$

NEGOTIATING THE TRADE-IN VALUE

Playing the Game to Win

Now let's dive into the topic of negotiating the trade-in value. This is where things get real and where those who are truly skilled at buying cars shine. With your research on the market value of your vehicle in hand, approach the negotiation confidently. This isn't a time to play it safe; it's a time to come out on top. Be ready to stand by your desired price and provide evidence to support your arguments. If needed bring in trusted experts like a mechanic or online reports to back you up. However, remember that being a car buyer also means being open to discussions and willing to make compromises when necessary. Utilize your knowledge and negotiation abilities to secure the trade-in value.

UNDERSTANDING DOWN PAYMENTS

Fueling Your Financing Power

$$e^{i\pi} + 1 = 0$$

Now let's shift our focus to payments. Consider them as the fuel that drives your ability to finance. A down payment is a payment made when you purchase something like a car. It reduces the amount you need to finance giving you control over your car buying journey. That's not all as a significant down payment decreases the loan amount. It also lowers your monthly payments and reduces interest charges. By recognizing the significance of down payments, you can enhance your financing capabilities and maximize your advantage during negotiations.

DETERMINING THE IDEAL DOWN PAYMENT

Making Smart Financial Choices

Pausing to scrutinize your fiscal health and objectives is key when deciding on the down payment. This understanding allows you to determine an amount that won't put a strain on your pocket as a regular expense. Remember, this serves as a stepping stone in claiming the upper hand within your car

$$e^{i\pi} + 1 = 0$$

purchase. A larger initial down payment may reduce your borrowing sum which could arguably tip interest rates and loan conditions in your favor. Selecting to put down less upfront money keeps more cash at hand however, it might raise monthly dues or total expenses in the long run. By carefully weighing options wisely you help to arrive at a healthy balance that is suitable for favorable rates and credit terms.

EXPLORING FINANCING OPTIONS

Aligning Down Payments with Loan Term

Now is the perfect time to delve into your financial options. Like a race car driver maneuvering through an intricate course, you must navigate through complex loan terms until you find one that suits your monetary goals best. Note that down payments can impact interest rates and overall loan

$$e^{i\pi} + 1 = 0$$

length as well as affect approval odds for loans themselves. But worry not as expertise in finance mechanics isn't mandatory to comprehend this process thoroughly. Devote some quality hours towards researching various financing choices available at hand. Grasping how precisely down payments influence various aspects of loans will significantly help you with decision-making during negotiation scenarios. It's time for your financing skills to move to the next gear!

KNOWING YOUR WORTH

Negotiating Down Payments

As a potential car buyer, it's vital to grasp your worth and discuss terms assertively, like an experienced automobile purchaser. Set aside time for probing market trends, interest rates and credit arrangements so that you can set reasonable goals knowing what opportunities are available. Keep in mind that you're not compromising but striving for the best possible

$$e^{i\pi} + 1 = 0$$

outcome. Always be ready to justify your proposed payment sum and lobby effectively for the best loan conditions. It's crucial to never sell yourself short! Being assertive during negotiations will always enhance your chance of success. Continue to establish yourself as savvy negotiator claiming your path on the road to victory.

Congratulations! By mastering the art of maximizing trade-ins and utilizing down payments wisely, you are accelerating your journey toward buying a car. By embracing the proven strategies of buying a car such as maximizing trade-in values,understanding down payments, determining a down payment amount, exploring financing options thoroughly, aligning down payments with suitable loan terms and negotiating down payments confidently, you unleash your inner genius when it comes to purchasing cars. Now it's time to put these strategies into action and apply them in real life situations.

$$e^{i\pi} + 1 = 0$$

Take charge and confidently navigate through the process of purchasing a car. Equip yourself with trade-in research of a vehicle and a clear understanding of how down payments can affect your loan terms. The path to buying a car awaits you. Get ready, step on the gas and make it a reality!

$$e^{i\pi} + 1 = 0$$

CHAPTER 9

THE POWER OF FINANCING AND WARRANTIES UNLEASHING YOUR INNER CAR BUYING GENIUS

$$e^{i\pi} + 1 = 0$$

WELCOME TO THE REALM OF FINANCING AND WARRANTIES

Welcome back my esteemed car buyers, to the compelling

realm of financing and warranties—a universe full of

opportunities and potential pitfalls. In this chapter, we will

$$e^{i\pi} + 1 = 0$$

explore the intricacies of securing financing and understanding warranties. Prepare to unlock the full potential of your car buying genius as we navigate through this exhilarating terrain together.

FINANCIAL MASTERY

The Foundation of A Car Buying Genius

Someone knowledgeable about buying cars and understands the influence of

expertise when it comes to acquiring a vehicle. Prior to delving into the realm of financing, it is essential to pause and assess your circumstances such as, your credit rating, income level and current debt responsibilities. Having an understanding of your position empowers you to make well informed choices that align with your budget and aspirations. Mastering your finances forms the foundation of your car buying journey.

$$e^{i\pi} + 1 = 0$$

SHOP AROUND FOR FINANCING

$$e^{i\pi} + 1 = 0$$

The Quest for the Best Deal

In the realm of financing, a car buying genius embarks on a quest to find the best deal. Explore multiple financing options including banks, credit unions, and dealership financing. Compare interest rates, repayment terms, and any additional fees or charges. Leverage your pre-approved financing as a powerful tool to negotiate with confidence and secure the most advantageous financing terms. Remember, shopping around ensures that your car buying genius is untethered by limitations.

UNDERSTAND THE FINE PRINT

Reading between the Lines

To unleash your car buying genius fully, you must become a

$$e^{i\pi} + 1 = 0$$

master at understanding the fine print. Read through financing agreements meticulously, paying close attention to interest rates, loan duration, and any potential penalties or hidden fees. Seek clarification on any terms or conditions that are unclear. A car buying genius is well-versed in the details, ensuring they make decisions with complete awareness and transparency.

EMBRACE THE POWER OF NEGOTIATION

Unleashing Your Inner Car Buying Genius

A knowledgeable car buyer knows that negotiation goes beyond just the price of the car; it also involves negotiating the interest rates, loan terms and any additional fees or charges. Utilize your research and understanding of financing options to secure a deal that aligns with your goals. Keep in mind that your negotiation skills remain relevant when it comes to financing. Embrace your expertise in buying cars and strive for the most beneficial agreement.

$$e^{i\pi} + 1 = 0$$

DECODING WARRANTIES

Protecting Your Investment

When it comes to the captivating world of car warranties, it is essential to understand the terms and conditions in order to tap into your expertise as a car buyer. Take the time to carefully go through the warranties, ensuring that you comprehend what is included, how long the coverage lasts and any limitations or exceptions. Moreover, it is prudent to conduct research on the reputation of the warranty provider so that you can be certain they are reliable and responsive. By unraveling the enigmas surrounding warranties, your skill as a car buyer ensures that your investment remains protected against repairs and expenses.

EXTENDED WARRANTIES

$$e^{i\pi} + 1 = 0$$

Weighing the Pros and Cons

When purchasing a car, it's important for a savvy buyer to carefully weigh the pros and cons of warranties. Consider this aspect by comparing the cost of the warranty with potential savings on repairs and maintenance. Additionally, think about how reliable the vehicle is, and what type of coverage its warranty offers taking into account your own risk tolerance. While an extended warranty can provide a sense of security, ultimately, it's your decision as a car buyer to determine if it's truly essential or simply an additional expense.

Embrace Your Inner Car Buying Genius

Congratulations car buyers! You have now embarked on a journey into the realms of financing and warranties, thus unlocking your inner expertise in purchasing vehicles. By mastering the art of management, diligently exploring different financing options, comprehending the details in contracts, engaging in negotiation tactics, deciphering

$$e^{i\pi} + 1 = 0$$

warranty terms and evaluating extended warranty plans, you have equipped yourself with the necessary skills to navigate through these domains and make wise choices.

As you progress further on your quest to become a car buying connoisseur, remember to trust your instincts, rely on your knowledge and listen to your inner car buying expert. The world of financing and warranties may seem intricate at times but as you are armed with the insights gained from this chapter, you possess the ability to make informed decisions that align with your objectives.

Stay tuned for our chapter where we will delve into the fascinating realm of car insurance—a realm where your car buying expertise will maximize protection while optimizing savings. Your journey towards mastering the art of purchasing vehicles continues, so fasten your seatbelt.

$$e^{i\pi} + 1 = 0$$

CHAPTER 10

THE ART OF THE CLOSE
SEALING THE DEAL WITH CONFIDENCE AND PRECISION

$$e^{i\pi} + 1 = 0$$

$$e^{i\pi} + 1 = 0$$

$$e^{i\pi} + 1 = 0$$

GET READY TO SEAL THE DEAL

Welcome back my car enthusiasts, to the thrilling realm of

purchasing a new car. In this segment we will delve into the

$$e^{i\pi} + 1 = 0$$

pivotal stage of the car buying journey—closing the deal. It's time to embrace your car buying expertise as we delve into the art of sealing the deal with confidence and precision.

OWN THE ROOM

Creating a Powerful Presence

As you approach the closing process, it's time to unleash your inner car buying genius and own the room. Command attention and respect with a powerful presence that exudes confidence and authority. Stand tall, maintain eye contact, and speak with clarity and conviction. Remember, you are the expert and the one in control. Embrace the moment let your expertise in buying a car shine.

ASK THE RIGHT QUESTIONS

Gather Crucial Information

Finalizing the closing process involves more than completing paperwork. This grants an opportunity to uncover knowledge

$$e^{i\pi} + 1 = 0$$

and set the conditions of the agreement. Use this occasion to ask questions that fetch data and elicit information from the salesperson. You should gain an understanding of their motivations so that you can uncover any fees or costs. Explore potential incentives that could work in your favor. The better you comprehend, the greater your ability to negotiate will grow.

HANDLE OBJECTIONS WITH FINESSE

Overcoming Roadblocks

Objections can be roadblocks to reaching a successful close. But fear not, because as a car buying genius, you have the power to handle objections with finesse. Address concerns with empathy, understanding, and confidence. Listen actively, not defensively, and provide well-thought-out responses that alleviate doubts. Use evidence, testimonials, or industry knowledge to diffuse objections and reframe them as opportunities. Remember, every objection is a chance to

$$e^{i\pi} + 1 = 0$$

showcase your expertise and move closer to sealing the deal.

NEGOTIATE UNTIL THE LAST SECOND

Squeezing Out Every Advantage

Never underestimate the power of last-minute negotiation. Even in the closing process, there may be room for squeezing out additional advantages. Review the final numbers and terms meticulously, ensuring they align with your expectations. Be prepared to negotiate further, focusing on any areas that may not meet your standards. Utilize your car buying genius to secure a deal that fulfills all your requirements while leaving no stone unturned.

REVIEW THE FINE PRINT

Protecting Your Investment

Before signing any documents, review the fine print with a keen eye. Understand all the terms, conditions, and warranties associated with the purchase. Evaluate any additional fees,

$$e^{i\pi} + 1 = 0$$

such as delivery charges or documentation fees, and determine their reasonableness. If anything seems amiss or requires clarification, don't hesitate to seek further information or request changes. Protect your investment by ensuring that every aspect of the deal reflects your agreement and aligns with your car buying genius.

CELEBRATE THE VICTORY

Revel in Your Achievement

Well done fellow car buyers! You've successfully completed the closing process and sealed the deal, like experts in buying a car. Now is the moment to bask in your accomplishment and commemorate your triumph. Take a moment to think back on the journey you've embarked upon, the insights you've acquired and the unbeatable bargain you've managed to secure. This significant milestone serves as evidence of your determination, strategic thinking and steadfast dedication, to becoming a master of navigating the world of car purchasing.

$$e^{i\pi} + 1 = 0$$

Unleash Your Inner Car Buying Genius

You've made great progress in your car buying journey. Traversing your way to mastering the art of closing the deal, you have truly tapped into your inner genius as a car buyer. From commanding attention in the room to asking questions, skillfully addressing objections, negotiating until the moments end and carefully reviewing all the details, you have confidently and precisely secured an agreement.

Remember that closing is not only about signing documents; it's about solidifying a deal that meets your needs and aligns with your vision. Stay true to your car buying expertise by examining every aspect. Congratulations on this triumph car buyers! Prepare for what comes as we delve into purchase strategies aimed at ensuring a fulfilling and enduring ownership experience.

Stay connected as we continue this journey together, empowering you with the knowledge the car insurance

$$e^{i\pi} + 1 = 0$$

equation to master the art of purchasing a vehicle and

unleash your genius as a car buyer!

$$e^{i\pi} + 1 = 0$$

CHAPTER 11

UNDERSTANDING THE CAR INSURANCE EQUATION PROTECTING YOUR INVESTMENT

$$e^{i\pi} + 1 = 0$$

$$e^{i\pi} + 1 = 0$$

This chapter of *"The Car Buying Formula: Made Easy"* will give you an in-depth look into auto insurance. It's just as essential to have car insurance as it is to have fuel for the car.

$$e^{i\pi} + 1 = 0$$

In this chapter, we'll cover the basics you need to know about liability coverage, collision coverage, comprehensive coverage, and uninsured/underinsured motorist coverage. Being knowledgeable about car insurance will give you the power to make informed choices and keep your vehicle assets protected. Let's get going and find out all about it.

LIABILITY COVERAGE

Imagine cruising down the freeway, enjoying the scenery, when you suddenly find yourself smashing into something. With you being at fault, you now have to pay the bills for medical care, while restoring the damage along with legal fees. That's where liability coverage comes into play. Liability coverage consists of two main components: **bodily injury liability coverage** and **property damage liability coverage**.

BODILY INJURY LIABILITY COVERAGE

$$e^{i\pi} + 1 = 0$$

This part of insurance financially protects you if you accidentally cause injury to someone. It also covers expenses, compensation for lost wages and pain and suffering. Keep in mind that accidents happen when we least expect them to and they incur unwanted debt while racking up huge expenses. Having adequate bodily injury liability coverage will help you sleep comfortably at night.

PROPERTY DAMAGE LIABILITY COVERAGE

Have you ever thought about the expenses that come with causing damage to someone's property? Whether it's a car accident or a serious collision, property damage liability coverage comes into play to cover the costs of repairing or replacing the other persons property. Furthermore, it can also protect you against fees if the affected party decides to take legal action.

$$e^{i\pi} + 1 = 0$$

COLLISION COVERAGE

Safeguarding Your Investment

Accidents can happen when we least expect it. This is why we have collision coverage! Suppose your car is damaged in an impact and the expenses of repairs or replacement are rising up quickly no matter who was to blame? Collision coverage will step in this situation and take care of these costs to help ensure that your vehicle is safe and secure.

COMPREHENSIVE COVERAGE

A Shield Against the Unexpected

Life often throws unexpected curveballs, and regrettably, they're not always agreeable. Your automobile might endure the misfortune of being stolen, vandalized or even consumed by fire; it could also be affected by natural calamities, plummeting objects or a random deer darting across your path on the road. This is when comprehensive protection proves its

$$e^{i\pi} + 1 = 0$$

worth. Such insurance safeguards your investment from non-crash incidents, thus offering monetary assistance for fixing or substituting your car amid unpredictable adversities.

UNINSURED/UNDERINSURED MOTORIST COVERAGE

While you may pride yourself on your safe driving habits, not all drivers exemplify such conscientious behaviors. Visualize being implicated in an unfortunate event due to the actions of a reckless driver who doesn't maintain appropriate insurance or has none entirely. Stay calm! Uninsured/underinsured motorist coverage is there for your support. This safeguard ensures that if misfortune strikes and either you're harmed or your car suffers damage owing to the carelessness of an uninsured/underinsured party, it's not solely up to you alone to foot those costs.

When embarking on the journey of purchasing a vehicle, grasping core elements of auto insurance should be given extreme importance. Consider spending time reading

$$e^{i\pi} + 1 = 0$$

through potential policies—not only talking about understanding them but also making sure they are perfectly suited, based upon your individual needs before opting for one—so that at no point will a lack of knowledge or unfounded beliefs create unwanted financial hazards.

As you venture on your path of purchasing an automobile, always bear in mind how vital it is to grasp basic car insurance components. Make reviewing and understanding your policy a primary task that aligns with securing sufficient coverage, suited for your demands. Don't let inadequate knowledge or erroneous beliefs put unnecessary financial risks at risk. Hats off! By decoding liability coverage, collision protection, comprehensive assurance, and uninsured/underinsured motorist backing scope, you've just elevated yourself closer towards mastering the process involved when buying cars.

As you are well-equipped now, navigate through this process smoothly ensuring safety from unpredicted

$$e^{i\pi} + 1 = 0$$

situations.

Bravo! Having unlocked the mystery of liability, collision, comprehensive and uninsured or underinsured motorist coverage's intricacies, you've made a significant leap towards mastering how to shop intelligently for your car.

Utilizing this insider knowledge allows you to confidently traverse through the vehicle purchases process while safeguarding your valuable investment from unpredictable events. Ponder on the fact that your automobile doesn't only serve as transportation—it embodies all dedication and triumphs in life. Hence, it is important to tailor-make its protection suitably. Await Chapter 12 where we will delve into post- acquisition tactics on securing optimum insurance rates and warranties, sealing up an intelligent approach towards buying vehicles and continuously letting loose upon unleashing those smart inner instincts!

$$e^{i\pi} + 1 = 0$$

DISCLAIMER: The information provided above is for general informational purposes only and should not be considered professional advice. Consult a licensed insurance professional or provider for specific details regarding your policy and coverage options.

$$e^{i\pi} + 1 = 0$$

CHAPTER 12

LET US EXPLORE POST-PURCHASE STRATEGIES - PROTECTING AND MAXIMIZING YOUR CAR BUYING SUCCESS

$$e^{i\pi} + 1 = 0$$

$$e^{i\pi} + 1 = 0$$

$$e^{i\pi} + 1 = 0$$

Why is this taking so long?
Motors
Finding my inner peace
SALES

$$e^{i\pi} + 1 = 0$$

In this chapter, we will delve into a crucial aspect of the buying process that is often overlooked: **post-purchase strategies**. The adventure doesn't end with the completion of the purchase. Instead, it's just the beginning. Employing

$$e^{i\pi} + 1 = 0$$

savvy tactics post-acquisition ensures both the protection and amplification of your automobile procurement triumphs. Therefore, let us explore the clandestine. Methods for maintaining impeccable car health and optimizing returns from your asset.

MAINTENANCE AND CARE

Keeping Your Investment Pristine

Create a routine to take care of your vehicle and stay on schedule. Stay on top of recommended maintenance tasks such as brake pad replacements and fluid changes. By following the manufacturer's guidelines and seeking the advice of reputable mechanics, you will prevent minor issues from becoming major problems and keep your car running smoothly. When it comes to maintenance, prevention is always better than the cure.

$$e^{i\pi} + 1 = 0$$

INSURANCE AND EXTENDED WARRANTIES

Perpetuating Your Protection

Automobile protection isn't a single transaction; it entails dedication. Constantly reviewing your insurance plan is crucial to confirm that it meets your requirements. As changes creep into your life, you may need to recalibrate cover limits or incorporate additional options. Plus, don't forget to explore different rate charts, as they enable you to glean maximum benefits from every penny spent.

Contemplate securing a warranty well to provide an extra safety net, over and above the default manufacturing cover. This could ensure calmness should hefty fixes be necessary in future times. Spend quality moments examining alternatives alongside selecting one that appropriates your requirements and budget.

$$e^{i\pi} + 1 = 0$$

REGULAR CLEANING AND DETAILING

Preserving Your Car's Shine

Your vehicle is an extension of your dedication to excellence and achievement. Keeping it clean and well maintained does not only preserve its appeal, but it also safeguards the paintwork and interior. Make time for washing, waxing and interior cleaning, to eliminate dirt, grime and potentially damaging substances. Additionally, consider investing in treatments like paint sealants and fabric guards to shield your car from factors and everyday usage. A cared for and tidy vehicle does not only provide a delightful driving experience but also instills a sense of pride.

ENJOYING YOUR INVESTMENT

Exploring the Open Road

Make sure you prioritize preserving and improving the value of your vehicle. Don't forget to enjoy the happiness it

$$e^{i\pi} + 1 = 0$$

brings! Take it on road trips, discover places, and create memories that will stay with you forever. Your car is not a means of transportation alone. It also represents your achievements and opens up opportunities for thrilling experiences and adventures. Savor the feeling of being in control, and behind the wheel, choosing destinations that genuinely interest you.

Great job! By implementing strategies after making your car purchase, you're elevating your success in car buying. It's important to remember that it's not about the purchase but it's also about safeguarding and getting the most value out of your investment. Make sure to include maintenance and care in your routine, regularly review and update your insurance coverage, keep your car clean and well maintained, maximize its resale value, and above all, enjoy every moment of the journey.

As your experience in purchasing automobiles increases, know that the potential to elevate your journey as

$$e^{i\pi} + 1 = 0$$

a car owner rests with you. Be sure to not overlook the following segment, where we'll delve into strategies for reaping the benefits of gaining leverage and experience while purchasing vehicles using the information in the text. Keep crafting the roads towards your accomplishments, and keep exceeding limits by continuing your path of pursuing perfection!

DISCLAIMER: The information provided above is for general informational purposes only and should not be considered professional advice. Always consult with trusted professionals and follow the manufacturer's guidelines in maintaining your vehicle.

$$e^{i\pi} + 1 = 0$$

CHAPTER 13

LEVERAGE YOUR CAR BUYING SUCCESS FOR FUTURE ACHIEVEMENTS

$$e^{i\pi} + 1 = 0$$

I've done
my homework
C Motors
SALES

Down Payment
Monthly Payment
$
$
$ $ $ $
Down Payment
Monthly Payment
$
$ $ $ $

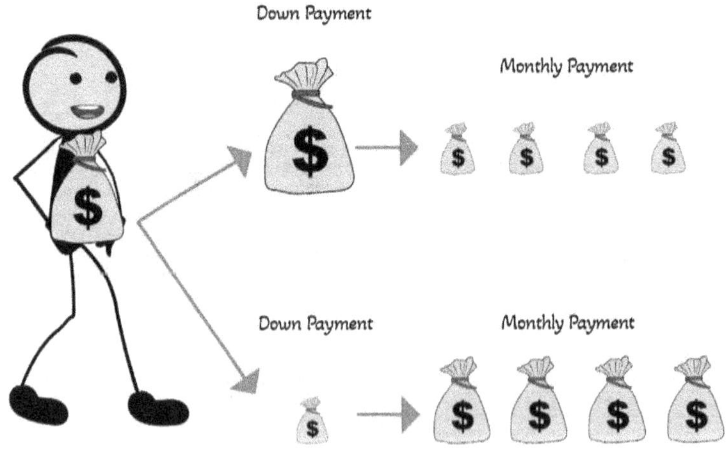

$$e^{i\pi} + 1 = 0$$

Now that you've completed the car buying process and obtained a vehicle that aligns with your desires and objectives, it's time to delve into how this achievement can set the stage for future accomplishments. Within this chapter,

$$e^{i\pi} + 1 = 0$$

we'llexplore strategies that can assist you in maximizing your car ownership experience and utilizing it to attain success.

RECOGNIZE YOUR ACHIEVEMENT

Celebrate Your Car Buying Victory

Take a moment to acknowledge your accomplishment in acquiring a new car. Appreciate your dedication and extensive research in discovering the vehicle at a price. Embrace the happiness and enthusiasm accompanying owning a car that embodies your progress and ambitions. This optimistic mindset will inspire you as you establish objectives for yourself.

NETWORK AND CONNECTIONS

Tap into the Power of Relationships

Your vehicle can be an asset for making connections and

$$e^{i\pi} + 1 = 0$$

networking with people with similar interests. Consider attending car events to become a member of enthusiast groups and participate in communities to meet individuals who share your passion for cars. By immersing yourself in these communities, you can gain knowledge, develop personally, and expand your network. Surrounding yourself with individuals who are passionate about cars and success will inspire you to reach more outstanding achievements.

VEHICLE BRANDING

Make a Statement and Amplify Your Brand

Your vehicle goes beyond being a mode of transportation as it also serves as an extension of your individuality and personal style. Think about adding decals, vinyl wraps, or custom accessories to your car that reflect who you are and what you stand for. You could also showcase a business logo. Conveying a message or customizing your vehicle will make a statement and draw eyes wherever you drive. This distinct

$$e^{i\pi} + 1 = 0$$

branding opportunity provides an opening for conversations. It can lead to exciting possibilities in both your personal and professional life.

UTILIZE CAR FEATURES: DISCOVER EXTRAORDINARY POSSIBILITIES

Modern vehicles come with features and cutting-edge technologies that significantly function to improve your daily routine. It's essential to take the opportunity to explore and fully utilize these capabilities. Whether it involves using voice control systems, navigation, or connecting your smartphone to access features, embracing your car's full potential will ensure that your drive is smooth and enjoyable. Stay updated with the features introduced by manufacturers and integrate them into your daily life for an enhanced driving experience.

UPGRADE AND UPSCALE

$$e^{i\pi} + 1 = 0$$

Progress and Success with Every Purchase

The adventure doesn't end there after you become the owner of your new car. It's essential to remember the potential for upgrading to a more excellent and prestigious brand or model as you advance in your life and career. Consider trading up for a vehicle that reflects your growth and achievements. By having confidence in yourself and aiming for things, you will ultimately reap the benefits of your hard work.

INSPIRE OTHERS

Share Your Car Buying Journey and Success

Embarking on a car-buying journey is more than an achievement. It's also about motivating others to seize control of their car-purchasing experiences. You can make a difference by sharing your story, knowledge, and helpful tips with friends, family, and fellow car enthusiasts. By becoming a source of information for those starting their car-buying

$$e^{i\pi} + 1 = 0$$

journeys, you can confidently guide them through the process. Your accomplishments can inspire others and empower them to unleash their inner car-buying genius.

Well done on finishing *"The Car Buying Formula: Made Easy."* Using your car buying success as a cornerstone for accomplishments, you're setting yourself up for even more significant achievements. Take time to celebrate your wins, connect with people, showcase your brand, make the most of the features in your car upgrade as you move forward, explore financial opportunities, and inspire others to follow in your footsteps. Keep pushing boundaries, keep setting goals, and never settle for anything less than extraordinary.

$$e^{i\pi} + 1 = 0$$

$$Ax + By =$$

$$e^{i\pi} + 1 = 0$$

$$e^{i\pi} + 1 = 0$$

$$e^{i\pi} + 1 = 0$$

$$e^{i\pi} + 1 = 0$$

$$e^{i\pi} + 1 = 0$$

www.ingramcontent.com/pod-product-compliance
Lightning Source LLC
LaVergne TN
LVHW020153070726
842527LV00018B/3964